Poems from the Waiting Room

Thomas Milner

These poems* are extracted
from Thomas Milner's blog "Notes from
the Waiting Room" written between
2011-2012, when he was living in a care
home overlooking the Atlantic Ocean
in north Portugal and dealing with the
consequences of multiple operations to
remove brain tumours.

*With the exception of *The journey
south* (1977), and prose extracts from
The Waiting Room,
published in 2011.

© Thomas Milner 2019
Published by

4₂

ISBN: 978-0-9957035-1-3

Poems from the Waiting Room

Thomas Milner

Life in the Lar I

My room has a view of the western sea.

I sometimes dream that I am running along one of those little streets just off the Rotunda de Boavista desperately searching for my parked car. I sleep in the north-south position and my three bamboo canes are arranged in a V-formation in the glass vase. So what am I doing wrong?

First extract from The Umbrella

I am an umbrella: just my luck. Reincarnation dictates a continuance of consciousness—the eternal "I" threading through time from the creation of the universe—that primal explosion of gas hurtling exponentially outward into the black vacuum of space. I am an atom, a child of Chaos, inhabiting now a wisp of gas, now a chip of matter, travelling for countless billions of years, riding the star-crowded waves of the cosmos. I have witnessed extraordinary things: I have seen the birth of wondrous worlds and their demise, flicked casually aside - the butt-ends of space. Thus I voyaged through the universe until I reached this place.

BEFORE (1977)

The journey south

And so we drove south
To the desert.
We climbed into the Aurés
Over shoulders of cork forest
Through warm, sweet-smelling glades
Of rotting trees.
(And rocks, grey rocks).
We turned and turned
spiralling up through a
Grey-green world
Until we came out high on a dry plateau,
Where range on range of mountains
Bore down from the west
As did those ponderous squadrons
Of squat battleships, teeth grinning starkly,
Bear down, menacing the Grand Fleet
In the Jutish way
On a Jutish day—
Something wrong
With our bloody ships
Today

And so to high Constantine
We came, perched on a gorge,
Guarding the southern pass,

A cold, dry, ancient place
Over which defeat and forgetfulness
Hung—the tatters of history—
And us, out of time and place,
Searching for a good hotel.
And if you asked me why I came
I would say that music drew me—
Sweet music - the chime and flourish of the carillon
Harmonic rhythms and Lydian airs,
That bore me into green hills
And syncopated my dreams.

Constantine the city was
Laid waste by Metellus and Beaufort
When the eagles stretched out their claws,
Grasping the known world, and
The Magreb, an eager jackal
Caught in my headlights,
Staring back.

And if you asked me what I heard
I would say Discordance, discreet
The sowing moans of the Lethargic,
The rasping, grating tension of the Bitter,
But not yet the bullet from the shadows,
Not yet the agony,
The massacres in the vineyard

And Casbah, not yet
The screams of the Damned.

Let us not stay in Constantine
For it is forgotten by the world.
Let us not stroll through the cold,
Grey, narrow streets
That funnel freezing winds
That buffet the upturned collar.
Let us not look too long on faces,
Blank with inchoate rage,
Numidian, Arab and Berber
Among towers of Roman classic
And French colonial.

Let us turn instead south,
As we did that day,
Descending through the Rhouffi Gorge,
(as we did that day)
Down and down we went,
Down and round and down
Until we reached the desert floor
And started to crawl.

THEN (2011-2)

I have a tree

I have an idea.
I have things, I have books, I have a son—I peeped into his book—he wrote about Galileo.
I have an old book about Galileo about the
    refutation of the accusation of the Inquisitors.
I have an idea, I have things,
I have an itch, I have notions.
I have a friend in China. She writes to me every
    year sending me pictures of China. Lin Lee is
    her name but that is all I know.
I have memories, which I select like cards slipped
    from the shoe.
I keep pictures from the past in a shoe box, slotted
    into decades.
I have a tree outside, slowly stirring in the early
    spring, its buds growing in the dark.
I have notions.

Birth entered the room

Birth entered the room
The tender wrapped thing,
Life
The inner quietness of exhausted birthing,
Shocked by the trauma of his passage
His smudged dark hair was damp against the cloth.
The little animal was nestling cold
Just starting out.

I knelt and peered in silent communication,
Love inchoate.
Then he raised his head
Oh my heart oh my son.
He opened sightless eyes,
Primordial, looked left and right.
Hello youngster, welcome to the world.

I read my book

After all the shouting,
After huge helpless explosions
Of coughing and sneezing,
After the angry scraping of chairs,
After the protesting screech of trolley wheels,
After clashing clatter of stacking plates,
After the cacophony of tossing cutlery,
After the moaning and lamentation,
After the shouting and recrimination,
The pink beauty of the evening sky
Behind the trees,
The mellow red-wine balm,
The zingy coffee-lift,
Restore my spirits and
Bring calm to this unquiet hall.
I READ MY BOOK.

I remember it well

All our notions and ideas,
All our fears and desires,
They pursue us down ever-narrowing rivers,
Down ever-decreasing fields of choice,
Ever-frailer bifurcations
Until we are left clutching at leaves,
Autumnal leaves ghostly and dream-like,
Fading and evanescent in the misty dusk.
I remember it well – driving along snow-driven
   moorland road, my headlights illuminating
   white diagonal swathes in the silence of
   that dark white night.
I remember the *jakes* at school, wet, cold and
   clammy and the four-hundred-year-old cedar
   tree on the ancient grass, propped-up by poles.
Poles Convent girls dancing with the pure-at-heart
   and that brown-eyed lady of the lowlands,
I remember her well.

When the going was good

Still a sad glamour clung to Travel in those days,
The coal-fire in the cold-stone waiting-room
Of a draughty Yorkshire branch-line station,

The 8.00 pm boat-train from Victoria
Rocketing through the dark Kent fields
Arriving at gull-shrieking salt-air Dover.

Orly at dawn waiting in the transit-lounge
For the tense flight across the glittering sea
And on to the hot sands of Africa.

I took advantage of my freedom.
I went when the going was good
And arrived at a dry stony place.

It beggars belief

A bowl of soup, a glass of wine
And thou beside me,
Ranting in the wilderness.

All the teachings of the Inspired Scriptures
Are dwarfed by the immensity
Of the star-crossed cosmos.

Pascal's wager need not apply.
Our vile bodies are consumed by fire
Urns of ashes towards sundown.

We therefore commit his body to the deep
In the certain hope that the sea will
Render him up on the Day of Judgment.

No sudden Epiphany brought me to this point,
Only the calm acceptance
That it beggars belief.

It beggars belief that we are all born
With the in-built virus of corruption,
Weighed down by some primordial guilt.

It beggars belief that our world,
Our wondrous awful world
Should blight our brief lives.

As flies to wanton boys
So are we to the gods;
They kill us for their sport.

At the hospital

We all stood around our father's body,
Laid out like an ancient Patriarch,
Unseeing eyes tilted towards acceptance,
Grieving.

Later I sat by the garden-waters and wept,
Remembering how he used to show me
His books, family treasures, one by one.

I then returned to my own place,
Tranquil in the hot season
Dry wind sighing through pine and eucalyptus.

But worming through the myriad-mazes
Of my dreams crept an uninvited guest,
The intimation of my mortality.

I'm homesick

Noise, noise, noise
Loud voices cracked and graceless
Bounce around the walls
Of the chamber
Of my damaged skull.
Irritation blurs my vision
Sunspots inside my eyelids.
I am depressed but I can't think why.
The figures wrapped in blankets slump
Lacklustre and inert, crouched to
Withstand some incoming stuff
The bombardment of imprecation
The barking tirades
The high whine of moral indignation
The boom of the opinionated
The squawking and the bluster
"Oh she's so stubborn, that one"!
(No, not stubborn, just old;
Old and weary and quirky
Just as you will be one day my dear).

After the skirmish the captain has a debriefing session with his Sergeant

- Well Sergeant, any casualties?
- Yes Sir; one Sir, Fernandes Sir, blanket-job Sir
- Was she *stubborn* at all would you say Sergeant?
- Ooh yes Sir, she could be so stubborn, that one!
- I see. Anyone else?
- Two others lightly injured Sir; they was caught in the-friendly-crossfire-of-verbal-abuse Sir.
- Jolly good; any other business Sergeant?
- Yes Sir, permission to request transfer, Sir!
- Good lord, Sergeant, any special reason?
- I am homesick, Sir.
- But I thought this was your Home, Sergeant!
- Yes it is, Sir, and I'm sick of it!

I am depressed but I can't think why
I can't paint, I can't paint, my hands tremble so.
I am demotivated shred by shred
And please witness the dismantling
Of my fragile self-esteem.
I am on the terrace now,
Soothed by the cold evening sun
And contemplating a misshapen cactus
Against a brick-red wall.
On the terrace
In my peace.

"Midwinter-spring is its own season, sempiternal
Though sodden towards sundown"
So I think, quoting the Poet, as I gazed
    through smoky chimneys
Then lift my eyes towards the open sea.

Chukran, Baby

I'm in free fall,
Recoiling back through the years,
Reversing back down city-streets
    and moorland-valleys,
Retreating from various hypotheses
    and bifurcations,
Shunning burning-pits and blissful-heights alike
Until I land lightly on my feet.
I'm a cool twenty again,
Young, green and full of hope.

Annaba: my first job.
Skulking behind grey filing-cabinets
Yearning for her black hair, olive skin
And flashing almond-eyes.
We exchange averted glances,
But it's just not on, old sport
Off limits, out-of-bounds
Strictly *verboten*.

Have to leave an hour early today,
J'ai Cour d'Arabe she explains,
Newly liberated from the hated French,
She's being Arabised.
That's cool, I think,
Chukran, baby.

White Petals

There was an old magnolia tree
    in the walled-corner
Of the garden overlooked by our school in Porto.
Every spring we marvelled at
    the white splendour of its flowering,
Its blushing blooms,
Its ethereal beauty.
White petals.

A vestigial planting from another age,
It was destined for the municipal saws.
When it was gone I was bitter-sad;
Well done, I thought, you got that right,
<u>Zero</u> for ambient aesthetics and
<u>Ten</u> for callous insensitivity.
White petals.

The cactus flowers on my terrace in spring,
Almonds blossom in the upper Douro,
But the paint explodes vermilion
Splashing onto my page
Slanting across my mind.
White petals.

Every night I drain the blood from
My hollowed heart
But in the morning
It's full again.
White petals.

My life is a canvas

My life is a canvas, once painted with broad free
strokes of the brush with a bold design of colour
and movement, now become crabbed and petty,
crouched into one corner, which is then enlarged to
fill out the vacuum left by my lost physical freedom.
Now and then the small things creep out from the
 shadows,
From under the damp stones,
Tiny lizards slithering out silently to bask in the
 warm sun.

Time hath, my lord, a wallet at his back,
wherein he puts alms for oblivion.
(Troilus and Cressida)

Why is Vladivostok?

Why is Vladivostok? When is Rome?
Where is Gdansk, when it's at home?
How many flies do I have in my ear?
Where are the snows of yesteryear?
Timor mortis conturbat me.

When does the Tagus flow so sweet?
Whence comes the heart at my feet?
How many fell at Sarajevo?
Whither the Euro?
Timor mortis conturbat me.

Which one's a coward and which brave?
Sean or Howard, Chris or Dave?
And the lords and ladies of Byzantium,
Where have they all gone?
Timor mortis conturbat me.

A spark to move my heart

A spark to move my heart
Catches fire
Incandescent flames burning
Flames of red liquid
Pumping central vermillion
Bloody, bold and resolute
Nerves jingling and jangling
My arrhythmic heart
Misses a beat
Galloping pulse
Stiffens, jerks and collapses.
Attack, fatal to my life's beating core,
Is my undoing and the hard floor
Rises up to greet me with its
Cold unyielding embrace.

Florence in the rain

> A friend of mine went to **Florence** to see
> **Bruce Springsteen** in the rain.
> She got wet, soaked to the skin, drenched,
> sodden, sopping, and doused out.
> But she felt uplifted, inspired, stirred,
> stimulated, moved and motivated.

Bruce was a blast
And looking fit
Though he couldn't last
Without his hit.
She visited some sights
Of that fair city
The *Duomo* was closed
Which was a pity.
However, she was able
To traverse the river Arno
On a bridge, old but stable
That's as much as I know.

Message in a bottle

Candy shoes
Running down the stairs
To greet the morning glory
Cherries are in season.
An old romance
Flickers in my memory
As I sit at my table
Waiting for the next course.
My eyes wearily sweep the room
Change and decay I see all around me.
Seeking solace I loose off a text into the void,
A cyber-message in a bottle,
Dipping sizzling
Over the rim of the World.

Her smiling face

The smooth face of a pretty young girl of eighteen
   is an untold story.

Before the heaving swaying voyage
Down the corridor of the years
Before the bounding intake of breath
Before the aching pangs
Of a bad romance

Before the striving
Before churning down the lanes
Of the waters of life
Before eye-opening knowledge
Widens her understanding
And travel broadens her outlook

The smile-lines at the corners
Of her honey-coloured eyes
Her increasing skills
Her gift of caring
All these blessed attributes
Will fill her cup to the brim.

Time, my Lady, in due season,
Shall trace its kindly lineaments

Across your smiling face.
But not yet, my Lady,
Not yet.

Sweeting's island

Captain Sweeting RN
Long since dead
Discovered an island
Whose people had existed
In harmony with nature,
Living in rhythm with the seasons,
Innocent and undisturbed,
Unpolluted with new ideas,
Uninfected with disease,
For ten thousand years.

Until Captain Sweeting arrived
In his little wooden warship.
Paused long enough to water,
Load the ship with fruit
And fresh vegetables,
Plant the Union Jack on a hill,
Update the admiralty charts
Before sailing away again
Into the great blue yonder.

Time enough for his men
To plant other seeds
In fecund wombs
Syphilis, plague and

The common cold.

I guess they were all OK
Before Captain Sweeting RN
Took care of them with his
Voyage of discovery.

The population of that island
Which had lain undisturbed
Since time immemorial
Was wiped out in a generation
And the rest is silence.

Second extract from the Umbrella

Being an umbrella represents a serious demotion—I must have blotted my copy-book quite disastrously in my previous existence. I'm being held high in the right hand of a young woman, my owner, who's using me presumably to protect her face from the sun. (Why pick on me, I'd whined to the *President of the Immortals*. He ignored my question. As an umbrella, he instructed me, your function will be to open and close, sheltering your owner from the rain or the sun: it's hardly rocket science; think you can handle it?)

The King of the Rainy Country

The sea is not calm today
The horizontal slash grey
With foreboding.
The swaying sobbing trees
The lightning flashes
The soundless arc-lights
Of distant strife.
A flock of small birds
Wheel in agitation
Against the dark sky.
A gust of wind
The hiss of rain
And the storm is upon us.
I snuggle deeper into my warm bed
And rejoice.
I am The King of the Rainy Country
Je suis comme le roi d'un pays pluvieux.
I exult that I have survived,
So far I have survived
I have survived.

Wake up and smell the coffee

So the neuro-zone is going down the tubes.
So our politicos are a dangerous combination
Of corruption and incompetence and
Every day is a good day to bury bad news
So our country is just one long beach
Where we become drowsy
With too much sun
So we grab any excuse to down tools
And close the factory to celebrate
A football fest
Innumerable saint's days
Municipal holidays
Political holidays
Traditional holidays
Long weekends
Mini-breaks ...

WAKE UP! SMELL THE COFFEE!

But no, on second thoughts,
Better let sleeping dogs lie
And besides, it's the weekend.

The touch of love

At the touch of love everyone becomes a poet
PLATO

I am an atom
A child of Chaos
Inhabiting now a wisp of gas
Now a chip of matter
Travelling for countless billions of years
Riding the star-crowded waves of the cosmos
I have witnessed extraordinary things
I have seen the birth of wondrous worlds
    and their demise
Flicked casually aside – the butt-ends of space
Thus I voyaged through the universe
    until I reached this place.

I was a tiny worm wriggling deep in the mud
    of the restless ocean.
I was a clam clamped to the wave-washed rock
Refusing to give up my secret.
I was one of the first marsupials to heave myself
    out the water onto the newly-formed land
Waddling with my fins up the primordial sands.
l loped and crouched semi-sapient and half-erect
    through the dark forests.

I was eyeless at the wheel toiling
    blindly with slaves.
I was one of the drunken Frankish knights who
    entered Jerusalem wading waist-high in
Blood.

I flew point in a V formation of wild geese flying
    across the Canadian uplands.
I was an eagle quartering the dizzy sky scanning
    the earth with my piercing eyes
Before diving onto my terrified prey.
I was a pearl diver, plunging down with my
    weight-stone into the murky green depths,
Forever seeking that glittering prize.

I was the leopard prowling
The rain-drenched gats
Of the Carnatic

I was a drop of dew
Garnered at dawn
In the Western Sands.

I was the blade
That pierced the side
Of the suffering prophet.

I was with my forebears
Crouched on the duck-boards
Of a Celtic-green trench.

I was the banner flouting
The northern sky
Fanning our people cold

I beat the warm thermals
With my featherless wings
I, Icarus, fell.

Extinct meat

Lunch today was roast dinosaur
Primordial chunks of meat
Inexpertly hacked from
Some monstrous haunch

I guess that such creatures
(Miniature pterodactyls)
Thought to be extinct
Are still reared for meat.

Bred in dark satanic pits
In the primitive hinterland
Of countries such as this one
And secretly distributed to
Mental asylums and
Old folks' Homes –
Institutions with minimal
Culinary ambitions and
Undemanding palates
Blunted by age
And misuse.

Yes, I suppose that's
The only possible explanation
For today's lunch.

Waiting for the results

Outwardly calm
Inward misgivings
Crawl up my spine
Coil round my neck
Worms of doubt.

Should be alright
Worse things
Happen at sea
Business as usual
Time waits for no man

But oh what joy
To freeze-frame the moment
And let the results go hang
At the edge of a dream
Waiting for ever.

Don't you just hate it when

Don't you just hate it
When that cheeky
Chirpy little guest
Uninvited but tolerated
Lodging in your attic
Weaving his nest
Hibernating the winter
Harmlessly slumbering
Unobtrusive
Unassuming
Unnoticed
Suddenly awakes!

Morphed into a
Lumbering bully
He moves down
A floor wedging His bulk
Back to the bone
Nudging and pressing
The complex software
The control pilot
The precious jelly
Of my brain.

And now the tender thoughts
The subtle arguments
Will be from my skull
Untimely ripped
And the interloper
Plucked out
Leaving blunted edges
And blurred prospects.

And don't you just hate it
When the breakfast cereals
Go soggy
In your
Painted
Bowl.

Wordlessly searching

Where would we be without speech?
We'd get by thanks.

Where would we be with only few words?
As a fallen leaf
In the autumn wind
Flabbergasted
Dancing and swaying
In the equinox
With no direction home.

Where would we be with no words?
Dished
Sunk
Undone
Helpless
Non-plussed
Stuck
lost.

Martian meteorite
(pops out for some milk)

You certainly took your time getting here.
Did you change at Clapham Junction?
Did you fail to get off at Kings Cross?
Or did you take the scenic route
Stopping to admire the way

The sun gilds Saturn's rings
With a chilly burnished glint.
Did you perhaps join the belt
For a few centuries?
(Did you remember the milk?)

There are still gaps in your story
The odd thousands of years
Unaccounted for.

Were you befuddled by solar gas
Or did you take time out
On some dark drifting orb
To ponder on the purpose
Of such a long voyage
Orbiting the question
Spinning like a coin
Pour la gorge

Did you have a crisis of Faith?
A cold realisation that the belief
You once held was a lie
When did you opt to drop the pilot
Splitting away from the main body
And decide to your own way
With no direction home?

And what were your impressions
When you finally felt the acceleratory
Tug of our gravity
And slammed,
A flaming fireball
Into our stratosphere
And fell,
An alien rock,
Onto our desert?

And above all what took you so long?
What time do you call this?
You've been gone for 700,000 years
For God's sake;
Too many cosmic rays
I'll be bound;
You even hit the wrong planet
Shame on you.

(And you forgot the milk).

Bark bark

Bark on, sister, bark on
At the aged creature who dithers
Listless all day in a mental fog
Who's queued all afternoon
In a gloomy crowded room
With a thousand years
Of spent humanity
Nodding off in front of
The stultifying crassness
Of daytime TV
Whiling the long hours away
In senile torpor

Suddenly whirled into tea
Mashed up dried biscuits
In an oversized heavy cup
Of milk or tea
Or milky coffee
Dunking bread
From time immemorial
Into the turgid liquid
Dazed and confused
Harried and hustled
Hectored and admonished
Muffled shouting

Hardly reaching
Into damaged mind
And broken memory.

Bark on, sister, bark on
But consider this:
Nothing divides you from them
But three odd decades.
Your present is their past
Their present is your future.

Quack quack

His mind is full of junk
Scraps of half-digested information
From third-hand sources
A dash of religious bigotry
Seasoned with cliché-ridden
Commonplace ideas
His understanding of
The planet and universe
Has inconceivable voids
His rare excursions
Into abstract thought invariably
Produce utterances both
Risible and ridiculous
In short he has the depth
And mental clarity of a
Small puddle in the road
And the intellectual weight
Of a poppadum.

Here a quack
There a quack
Everywhere a quack quack

(If there were a *quacking* event
In the Olympic Games
He would stand a good chance
Of representing his country).

Third extract from The Umbrella

Chrissie collapses me, neatly folding me again and again and puts me to sleep in my plastic cover. I dream again. I dream that I am a wind-hover riding effortlessly on the thermals. I am the heroic dog vigorously shaking myself dry scattering drops in all directions after rescuing the drowning child. I am the monstrous and deformed crustacean lurking on the deep sea-floor. I am one of the Norwegian banners flouting the sky and fanning our people cold. I am the fox-driven fire devouring the wheat-lands…

But I am only an umbrella protecting a girl from the sun and rain, which could be worse I suppose.

The texture of memory

The cat and the book
Bask together
On an old railway sleeper
In the warm sun
I feel the warm splinters
I smell the hot tang of the wood
I hear the cat purr
This is the sensual
Texture of memory.

I hear voices

I hear voices which caress
Like a breeze whispering
Across a field of lavender
In fragrant Provence

Alluring voices inviting me
To dally in shaded gardens
Being served chilled sherbet
On the banks of the Nile

Firm vibrant voices
Calling me back to the meadows
Where I ran riot in my youth
And dreamed of butterflies

Voices that pierce my skull
And jangle my bones
Voices drained through
A bucket of rusty nails

Voices that are like
Broken violin strings
Twanging back
Who strangled the cat?

Whining voices
Rasping voices
Truculent voices
Plaintive voices
High voices
Low voices
Strong voices
Weak voices
Old voices
Young voices
Nasal voices
Throaty voices
Voices from the past
Voices from the present

I hear distant voices prophesying war
I hear muttering in the mountains
And wailing in the streets

I hear clear well-modulated voices
Cogently explaining the
Dimensions of disaster

But most of all I hear my own voice
A lonely narrative
Echoing through
The chambers of my mind

A screaming rant
In this alien place.

Dream

I awake at tap on door
From an unfinished dream
already half forgotten
I reach back down
To clutch at the vestiges
Flailing after its tail
The beautiful symmetry
The perfect logic
The engagement
So good
Oh so right
Dreamworld in the
Subterranean labyrinth
Of my subconscious
The evanescence
Of my now totally
Forgotten dream
I'm left with a fleeting
Taste of regret.

Waiting for Sandy

The city braces itself
Battens down
And waits
Fearing the tide surge
When Sandy hits
He worries
His campaign flounders in
Wall Street awash
His concern is visible.

Meanwhile safe in Ohio
They make hay
While the sun shines
He urges them with repulsive lips
He nets them into expeditionary war
He can't believe his luck
Another ignoramus
In the White House

Sometimes I live in the country
Sometimes I live in town
Sometimes I have a great notion
To jump into the river and drown

Goodnight Irene, I'll see you in my dream

The end of the world

<u>21. 12. 2012</u>
For all seven billion plus of us
It's a win-win situation

A win because the magic number
Zero, three ones and four twos
Is predicated on an erroneous
Dating system
The Christian calendar.
(They made a mistake)

And also a win because I have
Something to say to all
The faithful and the faithless
The hopeful and the hopeless
Old and young and in between
Rich and poor and in between
Black and white and in between
Good and bad and in between

we who dwell in the slums of
Great cities
Green mansions
Country pastures
Wet Forests

Dry bush
Frozen tundra
Searing deserts
Flooded deltas
And the islands
Those thousand islands
This quote is for all of us:

This is the way the world ends
This is the way the world ends
This is the way the world ends
Not with a bang but with a whimper

T. S. Eliot – "The Hollow Men"

I wish I had a Sylvia Plath

I wish I had a Sylvia Plath
Mournfully sings Ryan Adams
On his best-selling album Gold.
I know exactly how he feels.
I too wish I had a Sylvia Plath
We too would drink Martinis
Very dry – three parts gin
And drink them
In front of a portrait of
Antonio Benedetto Carpano
The inventor of vermouth
And discuss her art and sullen craft
And how she became a legend
Converting trauma
Into triumphant and terrible words
And why she described Ariel
As a blood-jet.

And I'm sure she would agree
To me paying tribute to her
With her last prescient
And perfect poem:

The moon has nothing to be sad about,
Staring from her hood of bone.
She is used to this sort of thing.
Her blacks crackle and drag.

A good Friday

I caught a moment of truth
There in that old church,
Sitting remotely gazing
At the old carved gold
Of that quiet place.

My mind broke free,
Lifted and fluttered trapped,
Jerky and sorrowful, under
The fiddling fluted baroque
Of the Renaissance ceiling

The purple of childhood's
Dolorous Church
The stations of agony
Of English Gothic
The anticipation of Decorous Easter
Delicious costly scent of
Sculpted French chocolate.

Out again into the sunlight
On the steps of the old Convent
Church, I pause in that beauty –
The bright Portuguese light
The town below me

And the ocean gleaming over the trees.
Oh! Thank you for the day
<u>29 . 3 . 97</u>

Quotations & References

It beggars belief
William Shakespeare, King Lear

I'm homesick
T.S. Eliot, Little Gidding

My life is a canvas
William Shakespeare, Troilus and Cressida

Why is Vladivostok?
William Dunbar, Lament for the Makers

The King of the Rainy Country
Charles Baudelaire, Spleen

The touch of love
Plato

The end of the world
T.S Eliot, The Hollow Men

I wish I had a Sylvia Plath
Sylvia Plath, Edge